I0441773

BECOMING EDUCATED

The Options After High School

REBEKAH DAVIS, M.ED.

LifeRich Publishing is a registered trademark of
The Reader's Digest Association, Inc.

LifeRich Publishing books may be ordered
through booksellers or by contacting:

LifeRich Publishing
1663 Liberty Drive
Bloomington, IN 47403
www.liferichpublishing.com
1 (888) 238-8637

ISBN: 978-1-4897-0416-0 (sc)
ISBN: 978-1-4897-0417-7 (e)

Print information available on the last page.

LifeRich Publishing rev. date: 03/25/2015

CONTENTS

ACKNOWLEDGEMENTS

Thank you to Liz Nalagan, MA for the edits, suggestions, and input in this project.

Thank you to the many high school and college students whose struggles inspired me to write this book.

PREFACE

This book was written to help current high school students, recent high school graduates, not-so-recent high school graduates, G.E.D. holders, and their families make informed decisions about pursuing education after high school. Whether you earn a high school diploma or G.E.D., you have options as to your next educational steps and the choice is yours. The choice you make can impact the rest of your life, how much money you earn over your lifetime, the lifestyle you live now and in retirement, and the security of your family. Even choosing not to make a decision will impact you.

For example, Ben is a high school senior and plays football. He has been offered a scholarship to a large local university to play football. Ben understands that he has to maintain good grades in his classes to keep the scholarship and be active on the team's rosters. He needs to be honest with himself about two things: he is not good enough at football to become a professional nor does he want to and he struggles with several subjects in school. Ben realized that he will probably not be able to keep his grades up and play football, too. Ben chose to go to a local vocational and technical school where he learned to be an electrician and then was able to get a job that paid him well.

Sally, on the other hand, is very good at her school work and knows that she will have no trouble being successful in college. Due to her family's situation, Sally is not able to afford to go to college right away. Instead she takes a job and works full-time for a few years saving money for when she can go to college. When she does finally get to enroll in college, she will have to decide if she needs to keep working and go to school at the same time, if she can work just part time while in school, or if she can afford not to work while she is in school.

My experience of more than 10 years working in different colleges and earning my own degrees has taught me that many people do not realize how many options they have. It is hard to know what questions to ask and who to ask if you are not aware of all the options. My goal in writing this book is to provide this information so that you are able to make the best choice for yourself, your future, and your family.

INTRODUCTION

Whether or not to pursue a college degree is a question that most of us have had to answer at least once in our lifetimes. This question commonly arises for high school students, working adults wanting a promotion within their established career, adults returning to the workplace after an extended absence, and adults who have found themselves unemployed for whatever reason. No matter the category in which you find yourself, there is some information you need to know so you can make an informed decision.

The following chapters aim to provide much of this information enabling you to ask the right questions and to make the best decision for you at this time in your life. The great thing about post-secondary education is that you can start at any time and go back for more later! The scary part about making this decision is that making bad decisions can follow you and limit your options in the future. It is important that you have

1

all the information you need to make good decisions; sometimes the best decision is to make an informed choice today, and then revisit this decision after gaining some experience in the workforce.

LET'S DEFINE A FEW TERMS

Before jumping into the specifics about the options for education after completing high school or a G.E.D., there are three key concepts that need to be clearly defined. The first of these is what is referred to as *post-secondary education*. Post-secondary education applies to any degree or certification earned beyond high school. For the purpose of this book it also includes concurrent courses taken by high school students at either a college or vocational training center. Education or training for the purpose of employment that is completed in conjunction with or following graduation from high school or earning a G.E.D. is what this book refers to when using the phrase *post-secondary education*.

The next two concepts are the words used in the title of the book: *becoming* and *educated*. The use of the word *becoming* implies a process of growth and development into something greater. Think of the caterpillar that lives for a while eating and preparing to make a cocoon that will be the place in which it undergoes life changing transformation. Following a time of challenge and change, a butterfly emerges to live a very different lifestyle. The caterpillar was limited to the ground it crossed but the butterfly soars over the earth enjoying a very different view. This concept of changing and developing into an upgraded version of yourself is what is implied by the word *becoming*.

Stop here and consider this thought: If you graduate as the same person you were when you enrolled only having more knowledge, you missed the point. Anyone can learn anything they choose to learn by reading books or watching videos. Not everyone will take full advantage of the learning opportunity to develop into the kind of person who will be a successful employee and contributing citizen in society. Developing into a responsible and accountable owner of knowledge is a key component of a college education.

The last concept we need to discuss before moving to the following chapters is what it means to be an educated individual. Being *educated* applies to much more than the grades posted on your transcripts and the diploma or certificate hanging on your wall. The expectation of one who is educated is that they not only possess knowledge and the ability to find additional knowledge, but that they also think more creatively, critically, and with an open mind. Becoming an educated individual involves developing a new view of the world around you, a new perspective on overcoming challenges, and a new mindset about pursuing your goals and dreams. The institution in which you enroll is your place of challenge and change.

Pursuing post-secondary education is the transformative process an individual undergoes while learning the facts and skills needed to be successful in a career of one's choosing. As you read the following pages, bear in mind that whichever choice you make, you will be transforming into a professional with knowledge and skills that can be applied to a variety of circumstances. Ready yourself to be challenged and to find opportunities to gain experience. The old adage that experience is the best teacher is true; however, the wisdom to make informed decisions that guide those experiences is equally valuable.

A COLLEGE DEGREE OR
VOCATIONAL TRAINING
OR NEITHER

Many high school students choose not to pursue post-secondary education and that may well be the best decision for them at the time. Others, like myself, go straight to college because we are expected to but are not sure of the field we want to study. You may change degree plans several times and graduate with a degree you do not want. I changed my major so many times that my advisor suggested a generic "liberal arts" degree so I could graduate and figure it out later. I went to work for seven years before deciding what I wanted to study. I have visited with several people in similar situations. They have debt from student loans and a degree in a field that no longer interests them. You have options and one of them is to not pursue further education yet or ever. There are four basic options to consider when looking at post-secondary education: the military, vocational training, a traditional college degree and working for a while before you make a decision.

Before we talk about the education options, we need to ask a few questions about the subject or career field that you want to study. You might have favorite subjects in school but those may or may not lead to viable careers. You may have hobbies that you think you want to do for a career but may find that you do not like them near as much when putting food on the table depends on how well you do them. Determining your career of choice requires some self-exploration and awareness. What are you passionate about? What do you enjoying doing enough to do it at least 40 hours a week for the next 30 years? How much can you expect to earn in this career where you live now? Will you need to move to another city or state after graduation to make the amount of money you want or need to repay student loans? If so, should you move before you begin your studies? Which answers to these questions can lead to a stable career and secure future for yourself and your family? Experience and research will answer most of these questions.

There are a few ways to gain experience and help you answer some of the questions above. You may choose to volunteer or take a part-time job so that you gain exposure to the career you think you might want. If either of these are not options, you can ask if someone in that career field will let you shadow them on the job periodically. Talk to people who are successful doing what you want to do and ask them how they got there and what they would do differently if they could do it over. There are many ways to gain insightful experience while in high school to help you make the decision about which career to pursue or subject to study in college.

I also want to mention that you may not have to pick just one subject. Most colleges offer degree options that include a double major or a major and a minor. What this means is that you can earn one degree but have two subjects in which you have focused or specialized. For example, you might want a bachelor's degree in accounting but want to specialize in tax preparation or corporate accounting. Another example might be a degree in political science with a minor in history because understanding the history of American politics may help you in your political career. A biology student may want to minor in chemistry to better prepare him or her for a career researching ecosystems of endangered animals. Selecting a double major or a major with a minor will mean you take a few more courses which will cost more money and take more time to graduate. The advantages you may find will be in the career opportunities for which you may qualify.

One factor that may influence your career choice is the earning potential. Some careers offer more opportunities and higher earning potential in different parts of the United States and the world. To research the earning potential of a career, search online job boards (www.careerbuilder.com and www.glassdoor.

com) and government websites (http://www.bls.gov/bls/blswage.htm) that provide statistics about cost of living and salaries around the United States and in other countries. Depending on the career you choose, you might find it necessary to move to another area either before starting college or immediately following graduation. Be honest with yourself and your family about the possibility of moving away for your career; not everyone can handle moving away alone to start a new career, you have to decide for yourself. Now, that you are ready to explore the subject options, you also need to be aware of how and where to study them and the levels of college degrees and how long it takes to earn them. First, we will talk about the other two options for post-secondary education: the military and vocational training.

When considering the military for post-secondary education, you have to ask several questions of yourself before seeking out a recruiter to get more information. The realization you need to accept is facing combat; different branches see different amounts and levels of combat. Some occupations in the military may not see any combat. Another is whether or not you have an idea of what job you might want to do in service to your country and if it is a job that could be done as a civilian after you leave the service. Of course, you can join the military and select a training specialty later. When it comes time to pay for a degree, the military offers some of the best financial assistance programs like the GI Bill and Vocational Rehabilitation. Another option with the military is that you can earn a college degree first and then enlist as an officer to begin your military career. To explore these options further, meet with a recruiter and be honest about your desires, thoughts, and fears; you might want to meet with a recruiter from more than one branch, including the National Guard. Enlistment in the military could be considered vocational training but there are other options for vocational training outside the military.

Vocational training is an option for those students who want to get to work sooner making money doing a job they enjoy. Many high schools work with vocational training centers to allow high school seniors to attend both concurrently. The advantage to this is that you may be able to earn your certification even sooner and start making money. Even if you start vocational training after higher school or passing the G.E.D. exam, most programs take less time to complete than earning a college degree. Vocational training focuses on providing hands-on training to prepare students for the jobs they will begin working. This is ideal for those who prefer learning this way as opposed to learning from books; there may still be bookwork involved to complete training but the hands-on application makes this option more desirable for some.

Some of the most common vocational training programs include communication technology, auto and diesel mechanics, construction, child care, cosmetology, and certified medical professionals like C.N.A.s and medical assistants. While some vocations and some employers pay better than others, obtaining this type of post-secondary education may allow you to earn more than those employees who lack training and may help you to maintain a stable career. Many employers will also provide benefits for full-time skilled and certified employees. These career advantages may make it worth your time and effort to obtain training during or after high school.

The traditional college degree is an option that needs to be even more carefully considered. Earning a college degree may open career doors that the other options do not open but it is a more significant financial investment in the beginning. There are also a wider variety of degree options and colleges from which to choose. For example, if you want a degree in science, you will need to choose from options like biology, chemistry, botany, or environmental science. You might want to study technology, but what kind of technology? If you want to study computers, computer programming is very different than building the components that go into a computer. Each college offers different degree programs so you need to decide which degree you want and how far away from home you have to go to find a college that offers it. Be sure to explore your career field and the job requirements of the kind of position you want to help you determine which level of college degree you should work toward.

There are four basic levels of college degrees: Associate's, Bachelor's, Master's, and Doctorate. The Associate's degree is the first and generally takes about two years to complete. Some career fields will allow you to begin working an entry level job with an Associate's degree such as business, project management, or accounting. Hanging this degree on your wall may also boost your confidence and strengthen your momentum to continue your education even if you need to stop and work for a while before going further. Many students, like myself, attend local a Junior College or Community College to obtain an Associate's degree and then have the option of transferring to a 4-year college to work toward a Bachelor's degree.

Let's pause here to discuss how you might find a college near you or that offers your degree. Most Community Colleges advertise on television and the radio and will often mail fliers to addresses in neighborhoods close to the school. Definitely visit with your high school guidance counselor to learn about colleges in the area. You can also conduct an internet search using Google or Yahoo by typing college and your city and state in the search bar; for example, "community college Shawnee, OK" will bring up several colleges in the area. Be sure to carefully look at the search results because it will provide results for other colleges as well. Apply the same technique for finding colleges that offer the degree you want by changing the location to the degree, for example "community college electronics".

The Bachelor's degree can take an additional two or three years to complete for a total of four or five years of postsecondary education. Some students go straight to a 4-year college and work toward a Bachelor's degree; the requirements for graduating are the same whether you earned an Associate's degree first or not. Working toward the Bachelor's degree offers a more specialized look at the career field you have chosen. You may find these classes more challenging and more enlightening as to the career path you will eventually choose.

The Master's degree or graduate degree is not required for most career fields but is for some like counselors; it is preferred for teachers and many business professionals. A student must have completed or be working toward a Bachelor's degree to apply for graduate school. Most 4-year colleges and universities offer some graduate degrees but the degree options at this level are generally much fewer. Colleges and universities tend to specialize in their graduate programs and develop a reputation for being better than other schools for a particular graduate degree. By this time in your college career you have probably met some people who can recommend colleges and universities to you and you want to ask your professors. They will probably know better than anyone else which colleges and universities are the most respected in their field. You want to carefully explore this for two reasons: you might want to earn your Bachelor's and Master's degrees at the same institution and graduate school is expensive.

For example, earning a Bachelor's degree may cost $250 per credit hour while a Master's degree may cost $400 per credit hour.

The "credit hour" is the basis for determining when you having taken enough courses to earn your degree. Most classes or courses are three credit hours but they can range from 1 to 5 credit hours for a single classes. A one credit hour workout class will cost you $250 while the advanced biology class with a lab will cost $1,250 and require more time in class and more homework. The credit hour is also a way for you to tell how much work the class will require from you. You can see now why it is critical at the Master's level that you enjoy the subject matter of your studies and that you are able to focus on completing the workload. You will also find that many students at this level are working full-time and are enrolled in classes part-time. Working toward a Master's degree full-time often takes 2 additional years to the time you have already spent in college; studying part-time would then extend it to about 4 additional years.

The last and highest level of a college degree is the Doctoral degree, sometimes called the professional degree or terminal degree. You should plan on being a full-time college student for at least 8 years if you are planning to earn your doctorate. Some of the careers that require this level of education include medical doctors, psychologists, veterinarians, lawyers and judges, and college professors. For most other careers, a doctoral degree does not have to be earned before beginning work in the field. This gives you the option of earning a Bachelor's degree and beginning your career. Studying for a Master's degree and doctoral degree can be done on a part-time basis and may be done online to add convenience. One warning about online classes is that you miss the opportunity to interact with instructors and classmates and you must use self-discipline to get your work done on time. The reasons for earning a doctorate when it is not required for your career field vary among individuals. Some want to eventually teach at the college level to impact the newest members of the industry as a way of giving back. Others want to earn that status as an expert in a specific area to expand their professional opportunities. The expectation of those who earn their doctorate is that they focus some of their efforts on creating new knowledge that advances the field or industry.

Choosing the level of degree you want to earn is also often impacted by finances. The first and probably hardest part of deciding what to study and what level of degree to earn is exploring yourself and figuring out what you want to do as a means to provide for yourself and your family. This can be done by job-shadowing people you know, taking a part-time job, and volunteering. Talk to people who know you well and ask them what they see you doing for a career and why they think that about you. Research the careers suggested either online or at the library. The most important thing you need to do is be honest with yourself. I had a friend in high school that was told by a lot of people that she would be a great elementary teacher. I disagreed and so did she but not until she had spent two years in college studying to be a teacher. You have to spend time thinking about what you like and want and talking to people to help you determine what you want to do. Some people like me do not figure this out until later in life; I was 27 and for me it has changed again since then. Once you have chosen your college major, it is time to choose your college or university.

It is likely that you will find several schools that offer a degree in the field you have chosen so you will need to narrow down your choices before filling out the college applications. Colleges and universities are categorized in a couple of ways: public or private and not-for-profit or for-profit. All public colleges and universities are not-for-profit but private colleges and universities can be for-profit or not-for-profit; private schools can also have a religious affiliation or not. Each type of college or university has its unique benefits and drawbacks for different types of students.

Public institutions (a word that can mean college or university) are generally less expensive in terms of tuition; room and board for those living on campus is expensive no matter where you go. Public institutions often charge a higher tuition rate for students enrolling who live in a different state but some institutions have entered agreements with certain states not to charge this higher out-of-state tuition rate. Public institutions include those colleges that have the state in the name like Ohio State University or the University of Oklahoma and most community colleges. These colleges will state on their website that they are a public, non-profit institution.

Private institutions generally have only one tuition rate for all students. Private institutions can be non-profit or for-profit. Private non-profit institutions often have a religious affiliation either presently or in the past; as a result, they will usually offer degrees in religious studies. Their website will also state that they are non-profit and often have an area of the website for making donations. On the other hand, many for-profit, private institutions will not provide this type of information on their websites. They also do not usually offer living arrangements on campus so if you are moving to attend school you will have to provide your own place to live. Some of the most well-known private for-profit institutions include DeVry University, ITT Technical Institute, and the Arts Institute.

Another consideration in choosing where to apply is your high school grade point average or G.E.D. score. Some institutions will accept students no matter what their high school grade point average was as long as they graduated or have earned a G.E.D. Be sure to look at the entrance requirements of each institution you are considering; entrance requirements include having earned some specific credits in high school as set by the state and a minimum GPA or SAT or ACT score. The SAT and ACT are standardized exams that most students take while in high school; they cost a fee and are scheduled outside of class time. You can get information about these tests from your high school counselor or at http://www.act.org/products/k-12-act-test/ and http://sat.collegeboard.org/home. Specific degree programs may have additional requirements that can be found on the school's website.

Being aware of your academic ability will help you determine if you would benefit from starting at a community college to earn your Associate's degree before transferring to earn your Bachelor's degree. Community colleges are public not-for-profit institutions and they generally do not offer living arrangements on campus. If you start your education here, you probably want one within driving distance of your home. Many of the for-profit private institutions are also open-enrollment (the technical term for not requiring a minimum high school GPA). While their tuition rate is generally higher, these institutions are often able to offer smaller class sizes and more personal attention from instructors. This culture of student focus and attention is different on every college campus; visit the institutions that interest you and ask a lot of questions. Remember, you are planning your future and you have the final say in which institution will help you get where you want to go.

A third consideration in narrowing your choices for institutions is their accreditation. This is something that many students are not aware of but can prove to be either challenging or beneficial to their success. Accreditation is a means of ensuring that an institution is offering quality academic programs and that the students in those programs are learning what the programs claim to be teaching. It is important for two reasons: it adds intrinsic value to your degree and determines if your credits can be transferred to another college or university. Institutions who are accredited will post it on their websites and be glad to talk about it if you ask a representative from the school. It is most important to investigate accreditation when looking at private institutions. The easiest guide I can give you is to find out the name of the accrediting agency for the state institutions like The Higher Learning Commission (HLC) and then see if the private institution is accredited by the same one.

If you start your pursuit for a degree at one school and plan to transfer to another, be sure to ask both schools about the transferability of the credits you earn. It is most often beneficial to complete a degree before transferring but that still does not guarantee your acceptance at the next school or that they will accept all of the credits you earned. Just because you talk to an admissions representative does not mean that you have to enroll. These types of questions can often be answered over the phone not even requiring a visit to the campus. Much of this information may also be available on the school's website. You can talk to an admissions representative about entrance requirements like GPA and accreditation and transferring for further degrees without filling out an admissions application or committing to attend the institution. Ask questions and keep a record of the answers you receive.

So why do all of this work before applying to a college and finding out if you are accepted? Because most schools charge an application fee just to look at your academic information and determine if they will accept you as a student. Some schools also require resumes or other documentation in determining your eligibility to attend their institution or the particular program for you which you have applied. You do not want to pay application fees if their credits or degree will not transfer or give you the credibility you need to start your career. The amount of the application fees varies widely among the different institutions. Not all institutions will require an application fee and this may indicate that the institution will not have entrance requirements other than a high school diploma or G.E.D. Every student enrolling in college is different and has different dreams. Decide where you want to go and then determine the path that best sets you up for success.

Pursuing a college degree is not easy; it is a challenge in gaining knowledge, critical thinking, professional development, and personal transformation. It is worth the work and I challenge you to persevere until you finish what you start. The journey is as much a learning experience as the time spent in the classroom and in the library.

NAVIGATING ADMISSIONS
AND FINANCIAL AID

Once you have selected three or four institutions you want to attend, it is time to contact a representative and start asking questions. You do not have to complete an application to get your initial questions answered. It is the answers to these questions that will help you determine which college applications to complete. Ask about the accreditation and transferability whether you plan on going further in your education right away or after working for a while. Have them confirm the admission requirements so you are certain that you will qualify and ask about their financial aid and scholarship programs. Do not submit an application and pay the fee unless you know you meet their admission requirements and want to attend that institution.

Even after you submit the application and receive the acceptance from the institution, you still have time to change your mind. In fact, you have until the first day of class to change your mind without any cost to you other than the application fee. Once you begin classes, institutions have a prorate schedule concerning how much it costs to withdraw; there is also a paperwork process to withdraw that must be completed to minimize the consequences.

You want to begin working with financial aid immediately upon acceptance to determine the affordability of the institution; by this time you should already know the price of tuition and fees. You need to find out how much assistance and what type of assistance you will receive in paying for your education. Of course, in this discussion, I am assuming that you are not planning on writing a check to cover all of your educational expenses; if you or your family are able to pay for your education in full, you may not be interested in the rest of this chapter. You may, however, be interested in the following discussion on sources of money that do not have to be paid back.

If you are a military veteran, you will need to coordinate your benefits between your VA representative and a member of the school's financial aid or student financial services department. There are generally two options for funding your education as a veteran. The first is the GI bill and the second is Vocational Rehabilitation. Be sure to discuss your options with your VA representative and make sure you have enrolled in a school for which they will pay. There is also a vocational rehabilitation program available in most states to help non-military individuals pay for education. You can generally find out information specific to your state either on your state website or through the state employment services.

One of the first things you will be asked to do is to complete the Free Application for Federal Student Aid (FAFSA) at https://fafsa.ed.gov/. When you complete the FAFSA, you will be able to send that information to all of the colleges to which you have applied. You may have heard of the Federal Pell Grant, student loans and work-study; completing the FAFSA is how you apply for these programs. This application determines eligibility for these types of federal assistance based on personal and family incomes. The Federal Pell Grant is money paid directly to the institution by the federal government and applied directly to cover your tuition, room and board, and fees; this does not have to be repaid after graduation. Federal student loans are available in 2 types that will be discussed in more detail shortly but do have to be repaid with interest after graduation or withdrawing from school. The federal work-study program allows students to work part-time jobs on campus and receive a paycheck.

You can complete the FAFSA even before you apply to colleges. You want to complete it as soon as possible. The application requires information about the previous year's income taxes so you or your family will have had to file those, if required, before completing the application. The FAFSA usually begins accepting applications for the following school year in January. So if you plan to start classes in September you will want to complete the application as early as January of the same year.

Most states also have applications for students needing help paying for college. These are often awarded on a first come first serve basis so you want to apply early. Your high school counselor should be able to provide you with this information or you can go to your state's website. The federal and state governments are not the only sources of financial assistance for college students. Many institutions have scholarship funds for which students can apply. Be sure to look at the school's website and talk to your financial aid representative on campus about these.

There are many websites to help students find other private scholarships available to students; do not pay for a service to find scholarship opportunities for you. Two of the most common websites are www.scholarships.com and www.fastweb.com. Do keep a record of which scholarships you have applied for and any login information for the various websites. Check back to the sites often as the scholarships have different application deadlines. Spend the time it takes to use the free scholarship searches. Even if you pay for a service to find you scholarship opportunities, you still have to apply to each scholarship and may or may not be awarded it. I have yet to meet someone who paid for a scholarship service and said it was worth the expense.

Scholarships, like grants, do not have to be repaid, making them an ideal form of financial aid.

Grants also do not have to be repaid. The main difference between scholarships and grants is that it is generally more time consuming to apply for grants. They are often much more specific in who can apply but they can also be for larger dollar amounts than most scholarships. The Federal Pell Grant is often the only one for which students apply but search for free online. Grants can be a great source of financial assistance.

Now to finish our discussion on student loans. There are two types of federal student loans: subsidized and unsubsidized; you applied for these by selecting "yes" on the FAFSA question that asked if the student is interested in student loans. Subsidized federal student loans do not accrue interest while you are in college and for the first 6 months after you graduate or drop below part-time student status. Unsubsidized federal student loans do accrue interest while you are in college and you have the option of making interest only payments while in school. Any interest accrued while in school and the first 6 months after school is capitalized into your loan balance increasing the amount of interest you will pay until the loan is fully repaid. If the federal loans are not enough to cover your balance, private student loans are available for those with good credit and/or a cosigner who has good credit. These student loans require you to make payments while in school.

Consider these a last resort and pay them off first if you have to use them.

There is one other loan option that some families may consider called the Parent Plus Loan. This loan, if the student and parents qualify based on income and credit scores, allows the parents to take out a loan for the purpose of paying for the student's education. The money from the loan is sent directly to the school to cover any unpaid balance and the parents make the payments.

You may be asking, at this point, why one would bother with loans and just make payments to the school. The answer is that most institutions will not allow you to begin the next semester until the previous one is paid in full and no institution will release a diploma or transcripts of a graduated student if the balance has not been paid in full. Before you begin classes, you want to be certain the bill for your education will be covered.

When determining the cost of your education, you need to know that there is more than tuition to pay and books to buy. There are a variety of fees that will be charged to all students and there are also extra fees charged for taking specific classes like science classes that require use of the lab. Other courses will require you to purchase packets of extra materials besides your books from the bookstore. You will also need a variety of school supplies like paper, pens, highlighters, and notebooks. These additional expenses may not show up in your tuition charges but do add up to an unpleasant surprise if you are not prepared.

Another expense I have not yet mentioned is room and board. If you plan to live on campus you will be charged for your living quarters and usually a meal plan for eating at the cafeteria or food court on campus. These can be expensive and some students find it more cost effective to live off campus but then you have to be prepared to pay monthly rent and utilities and buy groceries to cook for yourself. Of course, renting a place off campus also requires you to provide furniture. Be aware that many institutions require freshman to live on campus for the first year while they adjust to life in college. My recommendation is to apply for scholarships and grants beyond what you need to pay your tuition, room and board, and fees so that you can set that money aside to cover these other expenses.

THE CLASSROOM

The expectations of your college instructors and professors is probably the one aspect of earning your degree that will vary the most among post-secondary education classrooms. Because of this, the following discussion has to be generic and is only intended to help you be prepared with realistic expectations as you enter your classroom for the first time.

Because pursuing post-secondary education is optional, instructors often expect students to put their full effort into the coursework and to complete assignments on time without being reminded by the instructor. Many instructors expect students to ask for assistance if they need it or to get assistance from other student support services on their own. Some instructors, however, will constantly remind students of upcoming due dates and offer additional assistance outside the classroom before the student requests it. It is likely that you will meet instructors who have expectations of their students all along this spectrum no matter which kind of post-secondary education institution you have chosen to attend.

There are a few things you need to know before entering the classroom for the first time. You will be given a syllabus that will inform you of school policies and your instructor's classroom policies. This syllabus may be emailed to you or made available through an online portal; if so, be sure to read it before the first day of class. The syllabus is also likely to include the schedule of topics that will be covered throughout the course. Some instructors will include assignment instructions and due dates as well. You, the student, are held responsible for knowing the information provided in the syllabus and conducting yourself accordingly whether that refers to behavior in the classroom or completing assignments and being aware of upcoming quizzes and tests without reminders from your instructor. There is also an expectation that you will spend about three hours reading, studying and doing assignments for every hour of time spent in the classroom. So if your class meets for one hour on three days a week you should plan on about nine hours of homework time per week for that one class. That syllabus is your guide to succeeding in the class but it is up to you to dedicate the time and energy to doing the work.

You are also expected to provide your own school supplies. Do not go to class without the textbook, paper, and a writing utensil at the very least. Nothing frustrated me more as a college instructor than students who came to class with nothing but their cell phones and expected to pass the class. This is actually quite insulting to your instructor. Be prepared to take notes and learn. Learning requires active effort on the part of the student; it is up to you to learn and earn a passing grade. It is not the instructor's responsibility to make you pass the class. Most instructors will provide additional assistance to those students who are making a diligent effort to succeed in class.

You may want to know how instructors decide who is making a diligent effort in class. First, we are fully aware of those of you who arrive late routinely. If you have a schedule conflict, a simple email or short conversation on the first day of the course will help you with this one. Second, come to class prepared both physically and mentally. Sleeping through my class does not make me want to help you. Be awake and rested as possible; also, read your book and do your assignments on time. Those students who come to class empty-handed are assumed to be uninterested which means the instructor will be uninterested in your success or failure. Instructors are people and expected to be treated with respect and common courtesy.

Most instructors enjoy getting to know their students and sharing their personal and professional experiences with those students. It is okay to greet your instructor in the hallway as you pass or stop by their office during office hours for a chat. Most instructors will tell you how they want to be addressed, for example, one instructor may want to be called Dr. Smith while another wants to be called Professor J. If you are not sure, ask. You may find that a particular instructor will be your greatest asset in the future of your career.

Earlier, I mentioned taking notes. I want to briefly share some additional thoughts on this subject. Some students master how to take notes in high school and some struggle with this. The most important thing about taking notes is that you write down key information needed to succeed on assignments and tests. The method for how you do this is not important. Do an internet search for note taking methods and watch some videos; try these methods for yourself and adapt them to help you learn. Some instructors allow students to record lectures. If this is not addressed in the syllabus, be sure to ask your instructor before recording any lectures. There are numerous apps for recording on smart phones and tablets; just be sure you are not violating any school or classroom policies.

The more difficult part of taking good notes is knowing which information is key. Here are a few clues. If the instructor takes the time to write it on the board during the lecture or discussion, you should write it down with any further explanation you need to know what it is later when looking over your notes. If the instructor uses a slide presenter and projector, what the instructor says about the information on the slides is sometimes more important so do not write down everything you see on every slide. Another clue is when the instructor repeats himself or herself, write it down. Some instructors will tell you that something is or would be a good test question while they are talking. A more subtle clue is if an instructors seems to get a little louder or more enthusiastic about a particular topic or part of the lecture. Each instructor will be different and it may take a few classes or even the first quiz or test to figure out what a particular instructor finds important.

Remember, notes are useless if you do not study them. It is best to review your notes from a class within an hour of class ending to complete any missed pieces of information while it is fresh in your mind. Some students prefer to take handwritten notes in class and then transcribe them into typed notes which is a great way to study them. Others prefer to type notes in class. Make sure your instructor allows laptops in the classroom; I had a few who did not. When using your laptop in class it is up to you to avoid the distraction of games and social media that might seem more interesting than the lecture.

Another area in which many struggle is managing their time. It is important to have a balance between time for assignments and studies and time for social and extracurricular activities. Keep in mind that you are paying for the opportunity to learn when you enroll in post-secondary education; it is up to you to do the learning with the tools and instruction provided. Plan time for completing assignments, reading and preparing for class, and studying for tests. Plan time for socializing separately. Many students confuse study groups as a time to mix socializing and studying and this is very wrong. Studying in groups helps many students succeed but keep study time and social time separate.

I have one more tip before we move on to learning that happens outside the classroom. Get, be, and stay organized! Even for those students who are not naturally organized, it is very important to keep track of your work. Keep work from different classes separate. Have a binder or folder designated for each class. You may find that information from a previous class is helpful in a current class so do not throw everything away just because you passed the class. The other advantage to organization is not losing assignments before you turn them in; when you complete the work, put it in the folder for that class and take that folder to class consistently. Staying organized in this way lowers stress because you are confident that you have what you need every time you go to class. Being a student can be stressful enough; being organized in school matters helps to lower that stress and keep you focused. For more on being organized, you might look in your local library for a book called "Organizing from the Inside Out for Teens" by Julie Morgenstern and Jessi Morgenstern-Colón or "Organizing from the Inside Out" by Julie Morgenstern.

In short, be ready for anything the first day you step into a classroom. As you progress through your education, you will learn what works best for you to enable you to succeed. Do those things over and over. Many of the skills you gain in being prepared for class will help you to be prepared for work like being organized, being prepared, being on time, being able to effectively interact with your instructor (who is like your future boss). Be aware of yourself and how the people around you and the decisions you make impact your success. Use that information to make choices that put you in a place to reach your goals and dreams. You are the only one who can make you successful so take advantage of the practice and experiences you have while you are in college.

LEARNING IS NOT LIMITED
TO THE CLASSROOM

As I mentioned in the opening paragraph, becoming educated requires more than learning knowledge; educated graduates are able to apply that knowledge in the practical setting of the jobs they want to pursue. The classroom is a well-designed learning environment but often fails to create the real-world scenarios for students to practice their critical thinking and application skills. At this point it is often up to the student to seek out opportunities to gain these skills. The types of opportunities a student might seek include: a part-time job, an internship, volunteering, and student organizations on campus.

Before continuing this discussion, we should briefly pause to mention that this kind of practical hands-on experience is one advantage that vocational education has over a college degree. Vocational education focuses on providing hands on training and experience that prepares graduates to readily transition into the workforce. Not every career that you might consider will have the option of vocational education so it is important that you know the value and the options for gaining experience before you graduate.

Whether you elect to become involved in organizations on campus, need or want to work, want to volunteer, or choose a combination of these, you need to understand two basic types of job skills: job-specific skills and transferable skills. Job-specific skills are those skills needed to complete job tasks unique to a position or field of study. To gain these skills, you will need to seek out opportunities directly related to the job you want to work after graduation. Talk to your instructors and the job placement office at the school for help finding these internship and job opportunities.

Transferable skills refer to those skills that can be used in a variety jobs to make you a more effective employee. Consider the following skills: customer service, cash handling or payment processing, phone skills, time management skills, the skills that help you stay organized and dependable. These skills and many more can be learned and sharpened at any job or volunteer opportunity. Realize that no matter the source of your experience, you can use it to become more valuable to your future employer by challenging yourself to grow within your current opportunities.

For many college students, working at least part-time is necessary. I have worked throughout my entire college career and during the times I was not attending classes. Some students find that they must work full-time jobs while in school full-time as well; it is doable but it is difficult. You must prepare yourself mentally for the long days and missed social events. The advantage these students have for working while in college is that they gain necessary transferable skills and develop the kind of responsibility and dependability that employers look for in new hires.

Ideally, a student would find a job that provides work experience related to their degree. This is not always the case, but if you get this opportunity, do take it. The long-term pay-off will be worth it. A part-time job in college could become your first full-time position after graduation. It could also create opportunities in which you meet people that could benefit your career down the road. Of course, for these benefits to become a reality, you must learn your job well and prove yourself to be a high quality employee.

If you do not need to work or are unable to work in your field, consider volunteering as a means to gain experience and professional relationships in the field. Volunteer experience is just as beneficial to you for gaining hands-on experience and practicing applying your classroom learning. Remember that while you are helping others through volunteering, you are also putting yourself in a position to learn new skills and apply what you have already learned.

Another opportunity that may be available to you is an internship. Internships may be paid like a part-time job or unpaid like a volunteer experience. Either way, an internship allows you to practice your skills under the supervision of someone already working in the field. Most colleges post internship opportunities with either the office of the dean over your degree program or with the office of career services or job placement. Your professors may also be aware of opportunities available so be sure to ask.

There are many ways to gain experience that will be beneficial to you while you are in college. There are three more things that make that experience even more valuable. The first is networking. Networking is the process of building professional relationships that can be mutually beneficial during the life of one's career. Some of these relationships may turn into friendships but generally the individuals you want in your network are those who are already successful doing what you want to do. You find these people through jobs, volunteering and other social events. There are social media sites that can help you stay connected with them but be aware of your personal social sites. When you are looking to build a career, social media can help or hurt you. Be aware of the potential consequences of your posts!

As you gain experience through work, internship, and volunteer opportunities, consider asking for letters of recommendation. A letter of recommendation is when a current supervisor or boss or co-worker writes a letter that can be given to any future employer during the application process. The letter usually discusses your skills and work ethic from the other person's point of view. Employers like to see what other professionals in the field say about your work ethic, skills and potential when choosing who to hire. Anytime you know you have done well, ask for a letter on letterhead. You will keep the original for yourself but include copies with your resume or job application when seeking employment which we will also cover in greater detail in the next chapter.

The most powerful skill and benefit of experience is reflection. Reflection simply means thinking back on your experience, particularly about your performance. What could you have done differently? Was there a better way to get the tasks accomplished? How did your attitude and effort affect those around you? How can you use this experience to become a better person and a better professional? You see, growing professionally is going to challenge you to grow personally as well. Keep in mind the explanation of the book title in the first chapter. No one is born a successful professional in their dream job. We all have to work for it; growing, developing, and changing are all part of the process.

EMPLOYABILITY AFTER GRADUATION

Employers are looking for a variety of attributes in graduates when considering who to hire. A completed degree is only part of the picture; it is great that you finished what you started and were able to pass the necessary classes. Employers are also looking for maturity and responsibility; they need to know they can trust the person they hired to do the job and do it right. Employers do not expect you to know everything or be ready for every situation; they expect you to be able to responsibly handle your work load and admit when you need help. Employers expect you to be accountable for your mistakes. They expect you to have a base knowledge that you should have learned in class and the critical thinking skills to put that knowledge to use on the job. With this in mind, it is time to start looking for open positions.

Finding job opportunities seems like it should be easy. There are several websites that allow you to put your resume on line and search for openings such as www.careerbuilder.com, www.indeed.com, and www.glassdoor.com. This is also a time to reach out to some of those professional connections you made while in school. They may know of openings or they may give you the kind of helpful tips that result in you being hired over other candidates. It is a common saying that finding the right job for you is a full-time job itself; you have to look on purpose and be diligent. Be sure to check in with your campus career or job placement office. They may also know of openings and have tips to help you be successful in creating a resume and interviewing.

A resume is the most common tool for applying for jobs when you have earned a degree or certification. I will give you a few tips here but this not intended to be a resume writing guide. A resume highlights your skills and experience that qualify you for the job to which you are applying not a list of every job you have ever worked. It is most often one page and not a page full of text; blank space in the formatting makes it more appealing to the reader and gives it a clean and organized look. Your name and preferred means of contact should be easy to find, usually at the top, followed by your education, experience, and skills that you have gained. There are many free templates available online and in word processing programs but that does not mean that they are all good examples to follow. Think about the employer that is going to read 100 of these to fill one job opening; would you want to read 100 resumes that look like the one you created? This is why it is important to be concise and simple in the formatting of your resume.

In addition to having a well done, typo-free resume, many employers require applications to be completed online. There are no shortcuts to this part of the process. Each employers' application must be completed thoroughly and accurately; many will allow you to also attach or upload your resume as part of the online application. It may be tempting to apply for as many positions as possible with each employer since you spent all that time doing the application but some employers automatically reject individuals who apply for numerous positions. Keep it to two per company; also, keep a log with the website, company, position applied for, and username and password information. Check back on each site to see if the position has been filled; again, you only want two open applications per company at a time.

Most companies will call or email you to schedule an interview. We need to visit a minute about the ring back tone and voice mail greeting they will hear if they call you. First impressions are critical and most employers are not going to be interested in hearing your favorite song while waiting for you to answer or your voicemail to begin; they might even hang up and decide not to interview you. Consider using a normal ring and simple voice mail greeting until you are hired for a position. The funny or sarcastic voicemail greetings that many of us record do not present the professional persona needed to get the interview and, ultimately, the job. Be mindful of the impression you are making on the stranger who might hire you.

Many of us have the habit of not answering calls from numbers we do not recognize but when you have put your phone number out there for potential employers you might want to answer those calls. Also be aware of how you answer the phone; answer with a simple and respectful "Hello" and maybe state your name. Avoid answering if you are half asleep or out of breath; remember they have not met you yet. You want the phone call to end with a scheduled interview.

This applies to email as well. Many of us create our email addresses with nicknames that lack professional ambiance. One recommendation is to create a separate email account for your job search. The email address should contain all or part of you first and last name so the potential employer is confident they are emailing the correct person. Also, since email is in writing, always use correct English in complete sentences with punctuation. You should always start by addressing the individual to whom you are writing (Dear Mr. Adams,), start your message on the next line, and end with a closing (Respectfully, or Sincerely,) and your first and last name on the next line. Remember, this person has not met you yet but is already deciding whether or not they might want you as an employee based on these phone and/or email interactions.

The interview is your chance to sell yourself to the employer convincing them that you are the candidate for the job with the most to offer the company. For most interviews you want to wear clothes a little more formal than what you would be expected to wear every day to work. Do dress in professional attire; an interview is not the place to wear tight or revealing clothing. Be ready with a firm handshake and a smile as you meet the person or people who will be interviewing you. Answer questions with confidence; it is okay if you take a few seconds to think through your answer to a question before giving it. Do not be shy when talking about your strengths and skills. Be honest when answering questions about your weaknesses; but discuss them in a way that indicates you are challenging yourself to improve in those areas of weakness. It is important that you show confidence in yourself through your answers and your actions.

The questions in an interview will range from questions about your previous experience, to what you know about the company to which you have applied for a job, to scenarios. The scenarios or behavioral questions usually present a fictional situation and you have to say how you would handle the situation. Listen to these questions carefully and take time to think about your answer. Answer honestly. Questions about your work experience will often focus on the skills you learned that will help you in the new job and may include questions about how your co-workers might describe you. You may also be asked questions that force you to describe yourself in a few words. What is your greatest strength? Answer this questions proudly and brag on yourself without exaggerating. What is your greatest weakness? Answer this one by also saying how you have learned to compensate for your weakness. For example, I am sometimes shy when meeting new people so I have learned to introduce myself first and ask a question to get the other person talking.

Getting the job is the hard part. Once you have the job, you will be able to prove to the employer that you were the right hire by doing your job well and asking questions when you are unsure about something. Be prepared for constructive criticism; this is when the supervisor tells you that he or she wants you do to something differently. Do not take it personally. Learn from it and keep improving. Any obstacle you encounter is a challenge and opportunity for you to learn and grow. Becoming educated does not stop on graduation day.

SO MANY OPTIONS

Several basic options have been provided so far. There are more options by combining the ones above. Think about the drink flavor combinations at Sonic®, you can combine the options I have shared with you in a variety of ways to create your personal educational journey. The four main options are attend college, attend vocational training, join the military, and find a job. Which of these you choose for your life and in what order you do them is up to you.

For example, you may know for certain that you want to go into the medical field but are not sure that you want to go to college. You can attend vocational training and pass the certification exam to start working or you can enlist in a branch of the military that will allow you to obtain medical training. If you choose vocational training, you will have to pay for it and financial aid may be available. You will also have to attend college at a later time to advance your career in the medical field.

If you choose to enlist in the military, you may be able to get all of your training and your education in exchange for your service. You could be licensed and ready to go to work immediately following your term of service. To stay with this scenario, you could also have earned your college degree and passed your license exam and then enlisted in the military. This option may still provide assistance in repaying any student loans you borrowed to pay for the education.

You might enjoy working with your hands and choose to attend vocational training to be a welder. Maybe ten years after starting your career as a welder, you decide you would like to move up and become the shop supervisor but that job requires a degree. You can enroll in college part-time and maybe online so that you can keep working while you earn your degree in business or management. Then you would be in a position to request a promotion at your current job or apply for a supervisor position with another company.

Your situation may be one that requires you to work right now. In that case, you may not be able to think about what you would like to do or if you would like to go to college. That is okay. Providing for yourself and your family is most important; in fact, that is the purpose of getting training or earning a degree. We all need to be able to make money and it would be great if we could be happy doing that. There may be a time in your future when you can revisit this decision and have the opportunity to do something different.

For many students, waiting to go to college is the right choice either because of circumstances, finances, or not knowing what they want to do for a career. A job for now may be the best answer today. Many of the skills like time management and being organized and dependable are skills that will benefit you on the job as well as in the classroom. Every job you work presents opportunities to challenge yourself to transform into a better version of you. Remember, that the options are yours and they are yours every day for the rest of your life. You can change your mind. You can change your path. Your journey after high school is yours to create.

A FEW PARTING WORDS

Obtaining education, whether vocational or in college, does not have to be a one-time event. You may choose vocational education and go to work for several years before deciding to earn a college degree. You may never decide to earn a college degree or get vocational training, either. American society needs all of us to continue functioning as we know it, but you are the one who has to live with the decisions you make. If obtaining post-secondary education requires you to take out student loans, are you willing and able to commit to repaying that debt? You may choose to work first and save to pay for your education instead. You might start working and decide that you do not want to obtain any further education and that is a perfectly acceptable decision. You may find a great job that you love but then find out that the employer wants you to obtain a degree or certification so you can keep your job. You need to know your options and decide if keeping the job is worth paying for and earning the education.

My challenge to you is to finish whichever path you choose to start at this time in your life. There is nothing more discouraging about your future than having to look back knowing that you could have and should have finished. Sometimes life does throw us curve balls and you might need to take a semester or year off from school to handle things but set a date to return to school and stick to it. You deserve the chance to reach your highest potential. Find people who have made it; let them inspire you to push forward toward your goals and dreams.

We all come to many crossroads throughout our lives. The crossroad of additional education may present itself more often than others. If you want to further your education, go for it and be sure to ask for help along the way. If you are not sure, it is okay to work while you decide. Pursuing education after high school should be a well-thought out plan and not a decision you make on a whim or in a hurry. Whatever you do, be happy doing it or it probably will not be worth the time, effort and money you spend.

ABOUT THE AUTHOR

I have worked in higher education for over ten years both on the business side of student accounts and as a faculty member. I can also honestly say that if I had known then what I know now, I would have made some very different decisions in my own pursuit of higher education.

In working with students over the years, I have realized that the reason behind many of their decisions, both good and bad, is a lack of information. Students take on a significant responsibility personally, academically, and financially when enrolling for college; yet so many enroll without understanding what will be expected of them.

I live in Oklahoma City, Oklahoma, with the love of my life. I am working on the last leg of my own educational journey in pursuit of a doctorate in education, which I am scheduled to complete in 2016.